Blended Family Momentum:
Secrets to Thriving in a Blended Family for Nearly Three Decades

Written by Michael R. Baker
& Brenda K. Baker

Other books by Michael R. Baker and Brenda K. Baker

Michael R. Baker
Finding The Titan: God's Formula For You

Brenda K. Baker

Helping Others Helps Me

The Ultimate Retirement Roadmap: Navigating Finances and Health Security

Also by Michael R. Baker and Brenda K. Baker

Moms Mixed Family Blender YouTube channel https://bit.ly/4fbtVA8

The Sedated Man Podcast
https://podcasts.apple.com/us/podcast/the-sedated-man/id1356865293

Blended Family Momentum Facebook page

©2024 Mike and Brenda Baker

Contents:

Forword

Dedication

<u>From Brenda to the Ladies</u>

Introduction

Chapter 1: Don't Sleep with Him

Chapter 2: Co-Parenting and Ex-Partner Interactions

Chapter 3: Building Relationships with

Stepchildren

Chapter 4: Establishing Blended Family

Identity

Chapter 5: Coping with Emotional

Challenges

Chapter 6: Managing Parenting and Discipline

Chapter 7: Maintaining Marriage Health

Chapter 8: Mothering & Emasculating your Man

<u>From Mike to the Men</u>

Introduction

Section 1.   Building Relationships with Stepchildren

Section 2.   Managing Parenting and Discipline

Section 3.   Navigating Co-parenting

Section 4.   Martial Relationship

Closing thoughts & Next Steps

Blended Family Momentum:

Secrets to Thriving in a Blended Family for Nearly Three Decades

Forword

Have you ever wondered why your remarriage and blended family seem to have all sorts of challenges once you got married, and you find yourself questioning if a blended family is really what God had in the cards for you? Or maybe you think that you married the wrong person?

In this book, Mike and Brenda will teach you how you got into the mess you are in, how to redirect the focus of your marriage and family, and how to thrive in your blended family long-term.

Not only have they been where you are, but they have also learned how to thrive for nearly 30 years.

Brenda has written to the ladies in the first part, and Mike has written to the men in the second part of the book. Although they have different writing styles, some of the stories are used more than once to capture the context. Mike and Brenda encourage you to read both sections of the book and then take the time to have open discussions with your spouse to communicate, regroup, and follow the suggestions that are shared.

This book is written for people who love God and want to honor Him in their marriage, for anyone who has tried to make their remarriage work but nothing is working, and for those open to learning from two people who have been at rock bottom and have done the work to have a thriving marriage for almost 30 years. Just because your remarriage is hard now does not mean it needs to be going forward.

Mike and Brenda have coached hundreds of couples on how to thrive in their remarriage using simple tips and tricks they have personally been using all along. They invite you to experience firsthand how simple remarriage can be when the right tools are put in place.

You can have a loving, connected marriage. All you have to do is do the work and never give up.

***Note: If you do not like references to the Bible or God, you will not like this book.

**To our boys –
Thank you for enduring the plan that God always said would work if people would only follow His perfect directions.**

Disclaimer:

Mike and Brenda Baker are not licensed counselors or psychologists and do not promote themselves as such. If someone in your family has mental or emotional problems, if there is abuse happening, or if you feel unsafe, Mike and Brenda encourage you to get yourself, your spouse, and/or your children professional help.

Blended Family Momentum is meant for people who feel something is off but cannot put their finger on what. This book aims to provide practical tools and advice based on what Mike and Brenda have experienced personally for almost three decades and/or helped other couples/blended families through. This book is not meant to replace a professional and should not be used as such. Mike and Brenda Baker disclaim any liability for any adverse effects arising directly or indirectly from the use of this material. Please consult a professional for specific advice tailored to your situation.

Introduction

Hi there, this is Brenda,

I thought you might want to know a little background on me, so here it goes...

I was born and raised in a small (at the time) town in Montana. I am an only child, and I grew up in the adult world. Not to say that wasn't good; it was just different than for other kids. We didn't live in a neighborhood with lots of kids, so I was around adults the majority of the time.

Both sets of my grandparents were my favorite people. I wanted to spend time with them any chance I got. One set of grandparents lived in the same town as us, and the other set was five hours away. I also had an "adopted" set of grandparents. They weren't biologically related; they were neighbors my parents became close to before I was born. Those six people were my favorites.

They all touched my life in many special ways. They were the reason I went into the nursing home business to begin with. I have a lot of love for the elderly. Had I not, I would never have been in the right place at the right time to meet Mike. God knew the choices I would make. He knew what I had been through and exactly the man I needed to help me become who He had made me to be from the very beginning.

God has a plan for you too. All you have to do is put in the work, and you can have a thriving remarriage and blended family too. That said, making changes can be difficult, so I encourage you to make the decision to follow through on what you've said you will do. Don't give in. Fight the good fight. Your blended family is worth it. ♥

Chapter 1 - Don't Sleep With Him

Have you ever wondered how people have a loyal and long-lasting marriage after divorce?

In this chapter, I am going to share with you the mistakes women make that keep them from having the very thing they want, how culture has influenced this, and how to get back to center if you got off course or how to get on the right track if you've never been on it before.

The goal of this chapter is only to provide a perspective you may not have considered. It is not meant to make you feel bad or judged. I challenge you to read the whole chapter with an open mind, seeking to understand.

If you know me in real life, this chapter was not in any way written to you. In the end, it is your decision, but based on all my years coaching remarried couples, there are many things that contribute to a remarried couple's success or failure, and this topic is one of them.

If you are a subscriber to our YouTube channel, you already know that I am a direct person. Part of the reason for that is I don't like to waste time. I want to help you get where you want to go. That said, blending two broken families into one that is connected and thriving is challenging. It takes a lot of effort and even more grace to get to a place where it resembles a family, but in the end, it is worth it if you are intentional.

There has been a lot of damage done to the traditional approach to marriage. It used to be that wives were excited to serve their husbands, and now our culture has tipped to "happy wife equals a happy life." I believe that the idea of keeping a wife happy as the easy way to a happy life is ridiculous. In my opinion, any husband who makes things easy for his wife and she has to do nothing in return but take is the best way to end up with a selfish woman.

Not to say that either side should have to do everything, but blending is all about give and take. Real relationships are a win-win.

My husband makes my life wonderful. He does a ton for me each day. He is a very thoughtful person, and he makes sure I know that my thoughts and feelings are important to him. I respect and adore him, and I do many things for him as well. What we have is a happy spouse and a happy house. It is a win-win. When we have a problem, we deal with it head-on.

We have learned that I need a little bit of time to process, and Mike needs things to be fully discussed and worked out quickly. It took time to figure out how each of us could get what we needed and still honor the other's wishes. But the point is we kept working until we found what worked. Our focus has always been to be on the same page, going in the same direction.

The main point is we both work on things.

I will be honest; most women have bought the lie that they should give sex a test run to see if it will work for them long term and provide a fulfilling sex life. This is absolutely not the way to go about a long-lasting, connected marriage, especially in remarriage. Giving a man privileges without being married is a recipe for disaster.

I've known many women who lived with their boyfriends, and honestly, each of them waited YEARS before getting engaged. One even had to move out to her own apartment before he would consider marriage. Ladies, I understand not everyone is interested in what God has to say on these matters, but the same women want to complain when things don't go the way they thought they would. What would you say if I told you that by listening to our culture instead of listening to God, you are creating your own misery?

Do you know why? Most men have no motivation to get married if they are getting all the benefits beforehand. To them, it doesn't matter. They don't really want to go through the hassle of planning and paying for a wedding anyway. Can you blame them? Weddings and brides can be a lot of drama.

Another reason men, in my opinion, don't want to get married is they believe that the sex is better and more frequent until you're married. Then it just stops…

Did you know that 67% of second marriages and 72% of third marriages end in divorce?

You are looking for physical closeness and an emotional bond, but what you really get is a man who has no reason to commit to you. Plus, you end up with a lack of discernment in the long run, especially those of you with a daddy wound. Having sex before marriage does not guarantee that the gap will be filled long term.

By filling the gap with God and giving yourself the love and appreciation that you are looking for, you will be able to test the relationship based on what you actually see in a boyfriend. You are much less likely to overlook issues. If he's not the one, you can move on and find someone else without the emotional baggage sex brings. Not to say breakups are ever easy, but clouding the facts will never help you long term.

Sex before marriage also makes women less in tune and aware of red flags when they present themselves. Three of the hormones released during and after sex are oxytocin, dopamine, and serotonin, which all create a state of attachment, making everything about the partner seem positive. In essence, you are setting yourself up for another failed marriage when you are not able to see problematic traits in your new significant other.

I can say from personal experience that if I hadn't been sleeping with my first husband before we were married, I may have seen who he really was long before I married him and had a child with him.

Did you know that there is a risk of damage to your immune system when you have multiple partners?

My point is, sex outside of marriage has many outlying issues that are not talked about. A relationship based on intimacy and attraction usually will not stand the test of time. It is kind of like paper in a fire. It instantly starts burning, but often before the kindling is burning, the paper has died out.

Furthermore, anytime you have kids in the house, you need to be cautious when bringing someone you've not known long into your house. Are the children safe with that stranger? Will he be nice to the kids when you aren't there? You just don't know.

Often newly single people forget that their children are watching. When you begin dating again, your children and your boyfriend's children will be watching. What example are you setting for them? Your decisions will influence your kids' decisions in the future. Do your very best to be the kind of example you want all the kids in the house to follow.

You might find waiting for marriage to be old-fashioned and outdated, but be honest with yourself, are you happy? Truly happy? I know I wasn't when I was newly divorced and single.

I honestly didn't find true happiness and peace until I found God. Sure, I was raised in a church, but I saw a lot of inconsistencies within the church, the doctrine that was preached, and the members. I remember questioning so many things as a kid. I wanted to be as far away from whatever that church said. Then I met Mike…

Mike has always had a way of questioning people (myself included) and getting them to think. As we were getting to know each other, I had many ideals that I had picked up, but those ideals were not serving me. Mike was good at calling those things out, saying something that made me think, and then changing the subject. He never belittled me or made me feel negative about myself. He just posed questions.

I remember one time in particular where his question pretty much burned a hole in my head for days trying to figure out why I thought what I did. This question led me to ask more and more questions about God until I finally asked him to study the Bible with me. To which he said, "no."

He had learned with previous relationships that I needed to study with someone else. So I did. Every day after work, I went to a lady's house and studied the Bible with her. On May 16, 1995, I committed my life to God through baptism. This was the first time I ever felt at peace as an adult.

Here's how to find God if you've never known Him before, you've lost Him, or you've been hurt by church people...

1. Purchase a New American Standard bible here https://a.co/d/iM5rnp2

2. Learn the way of Salvation according to the bible with Mike here https://bit.ly/3YHv76l
3. When you are ready to follow the steps contact us at info@blendedfamilymomentum.com and we will direct you to the next steps.

Chapter 2 Co-Parenting and Ex-Partner Interactions

Have you ever feared that the strained relationship with the exes will negatively affect your children and stepchildren? Or have you ever worried about potential legal issues or custody battles that would arise from negative interactions with your exes?

In this chapter, I am going to share with you how to minimize interactions with the exes and share some secrets that I used (and a few I wish I would have known).

My first interaction with Mike's ex was when I began picking the boys up from her for his visitation days. There were many reasons for me being the one to get them, the biggest of which was that his second-born son would kick, scream, and say he didn't want to go. This took a toll on Mike. Although he was willing to pick the boys up himself, I convinced him I was the one for the job. In my younger years, I was always up for a challenge. When we got together, his oldest was 4, the other was 3, and my son had just turned 2.

As you would expect, Mike's ex would play into the kicking and screaming and try to reason with this 3-year-old in front of me.

Obviously, I knew it was all an act. She was the one who conditioned the poor child to think that Mike was not his dad. So I would calmly say, "Get your shoes and coat on; we are going to see your dad." This whole escapade was just a ploy to waste as much of my time as she could and show me who was in control. And guess what... the exes in your life will do that too.

I have found personally, professionally, and when working with remarried couples that people always want someone else to blame for their problems, especially exes. Even if they were the one who did things that caused the problems or divorce, they usually don't remember that their actions were the reason. So get used to the idea that your ex sees your divorce as your fault even if it wasn't.

Why does it matter so much what your ex thinks? They are an ex for a reason, right?!

Did you do things that contributed to your divorce? Yes, you did. Were you part of the problem in your marriage? Yes, you were. We all are. Get the thoughts out of your head that your ex is or was the problem or was 100% to blame. Because once you are able to see your faults in your marriage and divorce, you are on the road to healing.

The best part about healing is you will not be hurting your kids or using them as pawns to get back at your ex. Taking responsibility for what you did or didn't do will help you not make the same mistakes in remarriage. Make healing a priority.

To be clear, I am not minimizing what you went through. I get it. Mike and I both went through some tough stuff during our previous marriages. Blended families all have a tough road. In my opinion, people make things much harder when they don't look for the things they need to improve on.

The secret to a happy remarriage while co-parenting and having ex-partner interactions is simple...

1. Keep co-parenting and ex-partner interactions friendly and to a minimum, especially when emotions are high.
2. Never allow the kids to tell you what the exes are doing, buying, or saying unless you have a reason to suspect abuse.

3. Train yourself to say positive things about your ex or stay away from the subject altogether. This applies even once the children you share get married. It may take time to get used to doing this without a negative tone or facial expressions, but in the end, it is best for your kids. If you love them, you will keep them out of it.
4. Train your kids' spouses not to share information, gossip, or repeat what exes are saying or doing from the beginning too, even under the guise of caring about you.

5. Keep financial matters to yourself. What I mean by this is never tell the children if their parent is or isn't paying child support or part of the expenses. It is none of their business, and I have found that children end up feeling angry at the other parent. Parental alienation happens easily.

Again, I get it. This list is difficult to hear. Some of these things I did badly. When Mike and I started our journey in our blended family, we didn't know anyone who was divorced. We were figuring it out on the fly. This is one of the many reasons we started a YouTube channel, wrote this book, etc. Learn from our mistakes and our successes.

If your ex has a history of being abusive or neglectful but is still in your children's lives, I would still suggest you work on the things on this list, but you do need to watch for signs they are being abused or neglected. Educate yourself on what those signs are. Put some checks and balances in place with the kids.

In my situation, Mike adopted the son I brought into the marriage, so we didn't have to co-parent or interact with my ex for very long. Which was good because my ex was very neglectful with my son. He only had supervised visits after our divorce when he did see my son.

Make it your goal to be respectful when communicating with exes and their spouses. If you ever do this badly, apologize. This can be super hard to do, but it is very important that you make every effort to get along. Side note, if the kids heard what you said... They deserve an apology too.

Lastly, if at all possible, have consistent rules between the households. One of the hardest transitions for kids is the back and forth and all the different rules from house to house. I am sure they always feel as though they are visitors at both houses, but this is made a little easier if the kids have generally the same expectations in both houses.

When we were sharing kids, there were times when the two households worked together, but for the most part, whatever we did, Mike's ex would do the opposite. Her goal was always to be a fun parent. She accomplished her goal at the time, but I am not sure it had the long-term effect she was going for. Most kids capitalize on the things the households disagree on and then use those things to stir up trouble so that they can do what they want.

Part of your job as a parent (stepparents included) is to hold your children accountable for their actions. If you are not doing that, I highly encourage you to start right away. Your children's futures are at stake here.

If you let a child off and don't hold them accountable for their actions, you end up with adult children who blame everyone for their problems or worse. I can tell you this from personal experience because this is exactly what ended up happening with our two oldest sons.

Mike and I didn't allow this crap, but their mom did, and as a result, nothing is ever their fault now. They are both over 30 years old and old enough to know better.

If the ex is trying to cause undue drama, do your best not to engage or ignore them. All you do is create more hardship for your blended family if you play into it or argue with them. Keep all conversation friendly and demote the ex from being able to call, text, or speak to you or your spouse in person if they are being verbally combative.

I know many people use different apps for blended families, so if drama is happening, keep all communication to the app until things settle down. Again, kids are much smarter than parents give them credit for. They understand things much better than they let on. So don't be fooled. Be the parent (stepparents included)!

Chapter 3 Building Relationships with Stepchildren

Have you tried to build a healthy relationship with your stepchildren only to worry that if you make any sort of mistake, your family will be divided and never reach a place of harmony or love?

In this chapter, I am going to cover what you can and cannot control as a stepparent, how to point out issues you see with your new husband's kids without causing marriage problems, and what you can start doing right away to support and be there for your stepchildren.

When I first met Mike, I didn't realize he had two children. At the nursing home where we met, I saw him with his cute little cowboy in tow often. One of the nurses I worked with encouraged me to talk to Mike and get to know him.

Since I am a pretty strong-willed person, I didn't listen. I waited and watched him. You could say I was a little bit of a stalker (when I saw him at work). What I was really trying to do was see who he really was.

I did not want another situation like I'd had with my ex. So I observed him. I listened to what he said when he talked to people. I watched how he treated his son. Once my research on him was done, I asked him out.

I think if I had realized he had two children, I might not have gotten involved with him. I am an only child, so I did not know what to do with them. I had a kid, but that wasn't going too well, so I think I would have shied away from Mike. At that time, I was defined by my past.

I had only been divorced about a year when I first talked to him. I was in an abusive relationship with my ex for over four years. He alienated me from my friends and family and made me question everything I thought and was told. I had trust issues before getting involved with him, and he made that even worse.

When it comes to building a relationship with stepchildren, at first you need to observe. Observing will help you determine what is working well and what isn't. Every parent has blind spots.

One of the main issues with blended families is the stepparent is usually the one who comes in and calls out all the spots the parent didn't see. Often the parent and the ex get their feathers ruffled. Even if their parenting isn't working, they will often attack your character or tell you that you are reading into things, ultimately trying to minimize the child's issues.

Another thing we see a lot is parents who make excuses for their kids' bad behavior or habits. Mike and I have seen these things specifically in most blended families we know or have been called in to help. I heard it said once that parenting is the most personal growth tool in the world, and I agree. Set a good example for your children. They will be who you are, not who you want them to be.

When you observe before you remarry, you are able to see what is really going on and determine if you are willing to work with those things. Trust your gut and be honest with yourself. This will save you from another
divorce.

If you are already remarried and you have experienced what I described above, I have some suggestions to get you out of the pickle you are in, figuratively.

1. You might see the problems, but do you know the whole story? The details in any family are important. So have patience. If you are in for the long haul, change your thinking now so that you can access the patience you need.
2. It will take time for the stepkids to want a relationship with you. Some of them will be easy to get to know; others will be difficult and even sometimes hateful. This is the part that is difficult because your efforts may be rejected now or in the future. You and your spouse need to come

together and talk about how these things will be handled. Your teamwork will help the blending of your family. In the future, if the kids go no contact, as a team you will be able to support each other.

3. Monthly, spend one-on-one time with each child in the house, even the ones who act like they hate you. Make the effort. Sometimes it pays off.

4. Do not skip your stepkids' events. You might think that it will reduce drama if the ex is high conflict, but skipping will cause more issues in

your house. If you go to your kids' events, have the same willing spirit and go to your stepkids' events. Be their biggest supporter. At the least, this effort will help build your relationship with your spouse.

5. Have realistic expectations. The age of the children involved will determine how long of a process this is. I know you want your big happy family, but you have to do the work to get that. Even then, sometimes you will not have it. Again, even if you are rejected, keep trying to build a relationship with your stepkids.

6. If you feel like you are being judged by your teen stepkids… you might be. The biggest thing to remember is they don't know what you know, specifically about their other parent (your spouse's ex). Don't take it to heart. Be kind when the exes come up in conversation. Do your very best to speak nicely about their parents or change the subject altogether.

At the end of the day, you cannot tiptoe around the stepkids. Nor should you. It is your house too. Do your best to love them in the ways they accept love and do not under any circumstances allow them to use or abuse you.

Having open communication with your spouse and getting their help and backup with their kids is one of the most important things you can do for each other. Often stepkids will try to come between you, but in the long run, your marriage will be the happiest and longest-lasting if you have a unified front.

Chapter 4 - Establishing Blended Family Identity

Do you ever feel like no matter what you do you cannot seem to unite your blended family? Or that your marriage is destined to fail and lead to another divorce?

In this chapter, I am going to give you some tips on how to help your blended family become more connected with one another and build strong bonds where each member feels they belong and are supported.

Many years ago, when we were so poor we could not afford to do anything we learned the concept of family identity. If you don't know us personally, we are some of the most head-first kind of people you may ever know. Mike and I both will put everything we have into following an idea IF we are convinced that it works like we are told.

When we first began having 'family day' we had rules. Those in the house were the only ones who participated, and we tried not to do the same thing every family day. Sunday was our family day. If the boys had friends who were going to spend the night, they had to be dropped off or go with their families after church. Because from the time we got home from church, it was officially family day. As the boys got older, we would allow friends who didn't have much in the way of a family to spend the day with us, and the girlfriends eventually did too.

Our initial goal was to make it a special time to bond. We'd play games, take family walks, go to the park, go on hikes, or watch a family movie agreed on by everyone. Some days, getting everyone to agree on one movie was a process.

As boys began leaving home, the rules on family day did change slightly to include adult sons and their girlfriend or wife and then grandkids. Honestly, some of my most favorite family memories are from family day.

We all got a chance to bond. As the family grew and changed, we would do geocaching and BBQ's. I miss those days now that we no longer live in the same place as our kids and grandkids. It brings me to tears wishing we lived closer still.

When the boys were young, we shared the two oldest boys with Mike's ex, so they were there every other week. Once we would watch the boys for her at any time she wanted to drop them off, we had them a lot more often. But even if the two older boys were not there, we still had family day with the other kids.

Another way you can build blended family identity is by everyone being involved in chores. Chores are a simple way for everyone in the house to share the duties of keeping the house clean and helping people learn to work together. In our family, when the oldest two boys were not there, either Mike or I would do their allotted chores along with our own.

Honestly, Mike usually didn't get a chance to help with chores because I was a stay-at-home mom, so I didn't feel right about him working 2 or 3 different jobs and then coming home and doing more work. Mike is an absolute angel, so he tried to help, but I usually had the chores done while he was working to be sure he couldn't help.

We always tried to ensure that the youngest two boys had age-appropriate chores where they could contribute to the family work but were also able to do them mostly on their own. I was always determined to make sure my boys knew how to cook, clean, and do their own laundry. It was my rule that all the boys started learning how to do their laundry at 8 years old. Sure, I would help them as they were learning, but I, as the mom, was not their slave.

I have seen a lot of stepmoms specifically coddle their own children but then be super hard on the stepchildren. I was determined not to do that. Unfortunately, my blindspot was that I was harder on my own children, one in particular. So here is my heavy warning against being harder on any one kid in the house. No child should ever be treated better or worse than any other in the house.

Favoring kids only loses connections in other relationships in the house. Sure there will be one you understand more, but don't ever favor them. Thankfully, I have made the apologies I've needed to with the one son I was harder on, but I did unintentionally cause him to be super critical of himself and a perfectionist. Some of that was his personality, but some of it I had a hand in too.

So again, if you tend to favor your biological children over your stepchildren, please stop this immediately. This will break any bond and ruin any chances of being close to your stepchildren in the future. It is one of the most unwise things I see blended families do.

One final way that you can establish family identity is to have family meetings. I don't really remember why or when we started family meetings, but they became a way that everyone in the family could bring up a grievance and ask for help with it.

I vividly remember two of our sons, who were not biological brothers, had been having a difficult time even being in the same house together for any reason. This specific time, I don't remember who called a family meeting, but the rest of the family had had enough of their constant bickering.

To make a very long story short, we all came to the table with suggestions on how they could co-exist in a better way. We all worked together to help both of them keep their attitudes toward one another more positive.

The faster you and your blended family can come together on a goal or project, the faster the process of blending can become. You may only have pockets of blending, depending again on the ages of the kids involved, but some blending is better than no blending. In the end, all these things really helped us.

Chapter 5 - Coping with Emotional Challenges

Have you or your spouse been undermined by the other bioparent, and you worry that you and your spouse will never be able to establish a healthy relationship with the kids and stepkids in your house?

In this chapter, I am going to share with you how to take the ex's punches while remaining calm and trusting that if the kids want to see positive things when they are older, they will. I will also give some ideas of things you and your spouse can do to stay connected and on the same team.

I will never forget the time that the sheriff showed up at our house…

It was one of the most traumatic experiences I'd ever had up to this point. Mike worked 45 minutes out of town, and I don't think he had anything but a pager at the time. I had no idea what they wanted. At first, when I opened the door and saw them, for a split second, I thought Mike had been in an accident or something.

My heart was pounding, and my whole body was shaking. The sheriff pulled out court documents and told me that a judge had ordered the removal of the two oldest boys. Although I was thankful nothing had happened to Mike, I was trying to wrap my mind around why on earth he was taking them. I was given instructions to have them collect their things quickly. There were a lot of things that I didn't really think about when the sheriff was there.

For instance, one boy had no reaction, and the other had a smirk on his face. After they left, I read the documents and found the boys were removed for alleged child abuse. This 'abuse' was not proven, but somehow the judge ordered emergency full custody to Mike's ex. This is one of the many problems with family court. The evidence and conclusions are drawn after the kids are removed. So much damage, broken trust, and time was lost with those two.

When it was all said and done, we were not allowed to see the boys or even talk to them if we did see them for 9 months. When the courts and a parent show a 9 year old that he has power he will do everything to keep that power.

The damage that was done during that time was substantial. When we finally proved that we were not abusing the children, we got to have the two boys back. There was a lot of stress because I didn't feel like I could ever trust the little turd that fabricated the whole thing again.

I will be honest and say lack of trust was a major struggle for me personally. I didn't want to be around either of them . I didn't trust that one of them wouldn't do it again. They were so spoiled and entitled that our family struggled to find balance again for probably 3 months after. I don't remember exactly the timing of everything, but all of it took a toll on both of us, but I would say especially Mike.

That said, my number one tip for coping with emotional challenges is to pray together as a couple. Anytime you are feeling down, pray. Ask God to help your heart heal and learn the things you need to learn so that you can come out of the 'trial' and be better.

A quote from Myron Golden that I love and really wish I would have heard back then is "That which is happening to you, is happening for you."

Mike & I were being taught how to overcome the next challenge we would face…

Next, pray together as a family. Invite the kids to pray if they want to or even ask if they have something that is bothering them, and then pray about that for them. If nothing else, it will make you feel better for a time. Slowly things got more normal for us.

Take time away as a couple here and there to reconnect and get away from the stress of things. When we were really poor, we would walk around and window shop at the mall and then share a dessert or plate of fries and talk. Those were some of the best times to talk and connect. Again, some of my fondest memories of our young years together.

I have never been a fan of therapy personally, but at one point, I did find an awesome Life Coach, and she really helped me to deal with some things and gave me useful tools to help me move forward. Honestly, she changed my life in so many good ways. So I would suggest a Life Coach if you can find one whom you can trust and who has good reviews from others. Also, one you can connect with. I would only suggest using a woman as well.

Lastly, I've mentioned this before in this chapter, but I feel it needs to be brought up again on its own point: keep open communication as a couple and as a family. This will help to bond all of you together, slowly. Children often feel that they have to be loyal to both parents, so this can cause issues, especially if you or your spouse make cutting statements about the ex to or around the child. So please guard your words and your tone when speaking of the exes. You are hurting your children when you don't.

There are many other things that you can do. These are just the ones that we put into practice that worked well. We kept at it and just tried to deal with things as they came up. Bonding & coping with emotional challenges go hand in hand. This is where you are able to communicate your care and concern for one another and be there for each other.

Chapter 6 - Managing Parenting and Discipline

How well the parenting goes or doesn't go is a clear indication of how much you and your husband are working together. In this chapter, I am going to cover the main pitfalls that come up in blended families when it comes to parenting and discipline, and how to express yourself without having the same fight about the same core issue.

In our 20+ years of coaching blended families, all of these areas are make-or-break points. They are also the biggest areas that people push back on. I guarantee you that if you dismiss any of these things, it will cost your marriage, your happiness or both.

Can we both agree that blended parenting is hard? Did you know there are ways to make things easier?

One of the many reasons I married Mike was he was super fair with my son and his two sons. From the very first time Mike met my son, he treated him like his own. He touched him in loving ways, was stern with him when he was misbehaving, and genuinely loved my son. I could feel his care and compassion.

Mike was never the type to lean away if my son was sick with the flu. He welcomed him into his arms when he got up from a nap or when he hurt himself. I have the utmost respect for Mike because he loved my son as consistently as he did his own sons.

My son was a challenging kid - the type who needed lots of direction. That didn't scare Mike at all. He was in it for the long haul. I, on the other hand, had a hard time wanting much to do with his sons. I never preferred my son over them, but I equally didn't know what to do with any of them. I can honestly say that Mike taught me how to love his sons like my own by watching him love mine.

A little over a year after we married, I had two miscarriages, and God used those experiences to help me see how important my role as a mother was to our children. Up until that time, I planned to always have a job.

After my second miscarriage and the death of one of my favorite residents at the nursing home I worked, it changed me. I vividly remember calling Mike on his beeper and sobbing when he called me back, telling him I couldn't work there and have my heart broken like that anymore.

Looking back, I was really grieving the loss of my babies too, but in true Mike fashion, he said, "Then quit". That shocked me because we had never talked about me quitting. Well, actually, Mike had talked about it, but I was adamant that I would never be a stay-at-home mom. Not long after, Mike told me he always knew I would want to stay home with the boys. I had no idea if I knew enough to stay home, but I felt the pull.

His two boys were in a day care all day, and my friend watched mine while I was at work, so at first, it seemed that we could make it work. But the loss of my income was hard on our finances. Not only did I have insurance for myself and my son, but I also had his two boys on my insurance. Mike worked one full-time job and two part-time jobs to make ends meet. It was a tough time, but I wouldn't change it.

Here are some tips to help you and your husband respect each other more.

1. **Anytime there is a disagreement, have it in private.** When dealing with a problem, talk to the child together. Being unified on punishments & discipline will help you bond in your marriage. It will eliminate the ability for the child to play you against each other and will bring security to the family.
2. **Expect all the children in the house to finish things like you do.**

3. **Expect all the children in the house to say they are sorry when they do something wrong to a sibling or to one of you.** When they do, make it a family rule that the person who gets the apology says "I forgive you". This includes you. The art of forgiveness has to be taught, and again since words are seeds, you are helping sow good seeds in your family.

4. **Make a list of non-negotiables when it comes to discipline & punishments together as a couple.** Discuss them in detail, and both of you decide how things will be

handled with the kids. Then follow that list to the letter. This will build trust with your spouse and the children because everyone will know mom and dad (in the house) are on the same page.

5. **Keep an eye out for bullying among the kids.** I am embarrassed to say I did not notice how much Mike's two boys ganged up on my son. He was the hard kid, so I mostly just thought that he brought it on himself. Oh, how I wish I would have looked into things more. Lots of damage was

done between those three boys that could have been dealt with.

6. **Do not ever, for any reason have a favorite child.** Favoring a child creates more blind spots. It isn't good for the children, and it won't help your marriage either.

7. **Everyone does chores.** The stepparent is not in charge of being the servant. If the stepchildren specifically are giving pushback, it is your job as the bio parent to bring the hammer down. By that, I am not referring to physical punishment; I just mean to let them know that you

will not let them treat your husband poorly ever and stand by what you tell them. Make them apologize to the stepparent and tell him what actions they are going to take to do better going forward.

8. **Be involved in the discipline with all kids in the house.** Be on the same team with your spouse, always!

9. **At holidays & birthdays no favoritism for any reason.**

10. **Expect the grandparents to treat all children the same.** Let them know your expectations, then give some

grace while they learn how to implement.

11. **If your children ever treat your spouse like a bank but don't want a relationship with them it is your job to put a stop to that and not allow bad attitudes or behavior toward your spouse or his children ever.**

All of this will also help to build family identity & trust too.

Chapter 7 - Maintaining Marriage Health

Did you know your marriage is the primary relationship in the house? In this chapter, I am going to cover how your marriage brings security to your children, even though your spouse is not the biological father, and I will give you some tips that have helped us still be best friends 29 years later (at the writing of this book).

On our YouTube channel, we get so much hate for this stance, and we will still shout it from the rooftops. Let me be clear: if you want your remarriage and blended family to work long-term, you have to do the work. Part of that is keeping the main thing the main thing.

Do your children need attention and love? Of course they do. But you know what they need even more? Security! Your spouse may not be the original dad, but they fill that role now. You've already shaken your children's security by getting divorced. I did too. The best thing you can do now is work hard and do everything you can to give them security.

What does that mean? Give them a loving mom and dad who love each other and sacrifice for each other every day. And work on that every single day, if you feel like it or not.

Early in our marriage, we began weekly date nights. We would switch who planned date night from week to week. The person who was planning would pick what we were doing. Occasionally, we would leave three of the boys with the grandparents overnight, on the weekend the older two were with their mom.

When we could afford to, we would leave town for the weekend. But in those early years, we'd just enjoy having an empty house for the night. On those weekends we dreamed and talked about what things we'd do when we were no longer raising kids. We loved our kids a ton, but we'd also, like you, never had a time in our marriage without kids.

Our rule on date night was we were not allowed to spend much time talking about the boys. We had to talk about how we were feeling, what we were working on, and how we were doing in key areas. It sounds very planned out, but all that to say we tried to focus on how we were doing as a couple. Sometimes we would talk about an issue that popped up that week, and there were a few times that date night was more of a chore. I would say that most every date night has been positive and helped us to connect.

Something else we always prioritized was apologizing to each other. This has helped our relationship immensely because there have been things that each of us could hold against the other. I believe with every fiber in my being that Satan is always trying to separate marriages using the mistakes we've made. Mike & I both have become very good at apologizing.

Taking it a step further when the other apologizes we have each become good at forgiving. I am not the most trusting or forgiving person. I will admit forgiving has at times been harder, but only when I want to be mad about something.

Mike is a genuine, good person. He is an excellent leader for me because I have huge respect for him, and he never tells me what to do. He asks a lot of questions to better understand me. I am still so grateful that I get to be his wife because he could have easily moved on when he found out that I am, at times, a lot of work.

That is another thing that I believe that has helped our marriage. I respect and trust him with my life. When we first got married, I would question him anytime he wanted to do something without me.

It took me a long time to trust that he didn't want to be away from me forever and he wasn't cheating on me... he just had something he wanted to do (usually for me). For the most part, I got over this and then when I was pregnant with the first son we had together, I struggled with thoughts that Mike wanted to leave me and find someone else again.

Pretty much the only reason I struggled with that was because my ex traumatized me when I was pregnant. So if your spouse is reacting to things that seem similar, give them grace. Find out things you can do to reassure them. Mike was very traumatized by his ex too. She had many affairs while they were together.

I quickly made it a habit to never have males who were friends. I went so far that I wouldn't let Mike's brother in our house if the boys weren't home. I would invite him to come back. I never wanted Mike to feel uncomfortable about me. It was always my goal to make Mike have the security that I wasn't going anywhere with every action.

Next, say nice things about your husband to others. Did you know that every word is a seed? In a blended family, there is already a lot going against you. A successful long-term remarriage will happen in your mind first. How you think becomes what you say. What you say becomes how you act. How you act brings closeness or drives a wedge. The decision is yours.

When you speak positively about your husband, that rubs off on the negative nancies in your life. If it doesn't, leave that friendship. Because if you aren't influencing, you are being influenced, and friends' attitudes matter.

Another thing about friends... if you have a friend or family member who is negative to or about your husband, move on. Again same concept as above. You are either influencing or being influenced.

It is YOUR job to protect your husband from your ex, your kids, your family, your friends, your parents, etc. If any of them treat your husband poorly, you need to make that stop immediately. I understand with your ex you cannot tell them off. I am not suggesting you do. But you do not need to stand there taking any crap off your ex either. That goes for your kids too. If they are disrespecting him, put them in their place.

I see far too many moms that have so much guilt about what the divorce did to their kids that they begin taking whatever low-level behavior their kids throw at them or their new spouse. This is not okay under any circumstance.

If you have already allowed some of this, my suggestion is get on the same page with your husband. Talk about things that have happened and how they were handled. Find out how your husband thinks those should have been handled. Figure out the details together.

Then call a family meeting. Apologize to your spouse in front of the kids, then apologize to all the kids, and have a hard conversation about how things are going to be handled going forward. If the kids have been allowed to have bad behavior, it is going to be a process. They may even try to control by threatening or even going to the other parents house for a while.

If you are able to communicate with your ex on the issues that have been happening generally. Then ask that your ex does not allow the children to avoid the issues or new rules by not coming over. Ask the ex to assist you by insisting they still come over on your parenting days.

If you are able, offer to do the same in return if something ever comes up in the ex's house and the child tries to hide out at your house. Those kids need both bio parents.

Just because you got divorced, that is no reason to allow the kids to choose sides or do what is easy. Relationships take work. I think it is always better for the kids if they are expected to see both and work through problems.

This is something I believe Mike and I did badly. Our oldest two sons were opposites. One was very much a mama's boy (with Mike's ex) and really leaned toward her, frankly because he was more on the physically lazy side and things were easier for him at her house.

The other was more connected with dad. What we didn't understand at the time was that he was emotionally lazy. He would take the easy way out on most every emotional thing. He would push it aside and not deal with it.

For example when Mike left for Iraq on his first deployment, we let this son go to a different state with our best friend. We thought it would be a good time for him to connect with our friend, who was like an uncle to our kids.

What ended up happening is this son didn't see dad leave on the plane. He didn't have to deal with how many tears I shed, his brothers shed, and the other wives, girlfriends and families shed. There was even one little girl who was screaming

"Daddy don't go" as the bus left the armory parking lot. It would have been good for this son. He couldn't have been emotionally lazy; he would have had to deal with it. But he wasn't there... and so for 18 months this son tricked his mind and didn't deal.

There have been many other situations since then and this son still doesn't deal. It has been a huge negative in his life, and I hope someday he will take the time and work through those things. But given his track record, I doubt if he will.

We could have avoided his emotional laziness if we had realized how important these things were at the time. The other son, who was physically lazy stopped coming over soon after Mike left for Iraq. Honestly, his mom encouraged it.

When Mike came home on a two-week leave from Iraq, that son decided he no longer wanted to be at our house at all. And let's just say he declined in behavior after that. Because he was allowed to stop what didn't serve him, he has been hateful and mean toward me at first and now toward the three brothers and

Mike as well. It is very sad because we loved him & sacrificed a lot for both of those boys.

Just understand things may not turn out the way you think they will. That doesn't mean you did everything wrong. Leave space in your heart to welcome the children who go no contact back if they ever decide to.

Make time for sex. We all get busy, but remember your husband is motivated by sex. I know women usually find it silly, but this is just the way your husband was built. It is not just how they feel physically;

it is the closeness and bonding with you that he is after.

Flirt with him, initiate sometimes, and be sure you are setting boundaries with your kids so that you and your husband are able to privately have this time together without fear the kids will hear or walk in.

I think a lot of women forget that God gave sex to bond you and your husband together. Mike and I tend to bicker a bit when we aren't as active in that area as we usually are.

This will be an area you will have to work on and have open communication with your husband about when you begin perimenopause. I have had a heck of a time holding myself accountable and finding solutions to help with this once I began perimenopause. Mostly because I did not want to be on meds.

One thing I have really found to work well for me is the carnivore diet. It helped me balance my hormones to the point where I was able to find relief without hormone replacement therapy. Obviously, every woman's body is different, but my only point is to be willing to seek help and get answers sooner than later. Your marriage depends on it.

Lastly, I feel the need to mention here: never, ever use sex as a way to get back at or as a way to get what you want from your husband. I don't think there are many other things that get the same reaction from men no matter what their personality.

Chapter 8 – Mothering & Emasculating Your Man

Has your remarriage ever felt like your first marriage where, all you ever do is….everything?

In this chapter, I am going to share with you the main reason most women mother and/or emasculate their husbands and ways to change that behavior quickly.

When Mike's ex was married to her third husband, there were problems. I don't remember how or why, but we were getting along at the time, and we were asked to help them. So, we'd go to their house and do marriage coaching with them, trying to help them stay together because they had two daughters together.

By the end of the second meeting, we could see what the main problems were. He was tired of her constant controlling and emasculating. She was tired of his lack of follow-through. She wanted a leader until it got in the way of doing what she wanted, and then she wanted control back.

Honestly, when we were on the way to these coaching sessions, we would pray that we would keep the past in the past and lean on God to give the wisdom and words needed.

It was a stretch for both of us, but we trusted that God had a plan. Mike's ex would go into all the issues she had with this husband, and the more she talked, the more he scooted down in the couch. It was sad.

Obviously, Mike knew from being married to her that as soon as something went different than what she wanted or she was challenged, she would bring up all the things he'd done wrong… ever.

Overall, the marriage coaching sessions we have done with couples, the number one problem we've consistently seen in women is they either mother or emasculate their husbands on a regular basis without even realizing it.

Think about it, when a mother is holding her child to a standard, what does she do? She watches very closely at every detail to ensure that the child is doing what she expects. In child-rearing, this is a very important stage with younger children. You must take the time to teach them how to do things well, and then once they do that, you teach them to be consistent and hold themselves accountable.

When it comes to your husband, that is not up to you. He is an adult. If you have a preference, talk with him about how you'd like it done, but if you want him to do things, you have to give him the ability to do them without being over his shoulder.

If you feel you have to mother him, it is time to roll up your sleeves together and get to the bottom of why. Then come up with solutions that both of you agree on moving forward. I find that many women either nag their husbands about things or they expect to say things once and their husband will do them. Neither one works.

I can tell you that often women see their husband as not as smart as themselves, or they feel their husband depends on them too much. So which is it for you? Most men will allow their wives to do everything if their wife just does it. I believe that is one of the many reasons that God has put men in charge of leading the household.

Now you can believe that or not believe it, but you cannot deny that if given a choice men will choose the path of least resistance. Part of that is our culture. Part of that is how we women react and take over. Just to be clear, please understand I am not saying it is right for men to do this. I am simply saying here is why.

The strong-willed person that I was in our younger years is much different than the strong-willed person I am today. I have learned that it is unwise for me to take over because I honestly cannot handle the pressure. Mike does a great job, and I trust him.

When Mike was in Iraq the second time for 12 months, we had a business, an employee, I was homeschooling 3 of our 5 boys, doing all the business things, being mom and dad, leaving the church where I became a Christian, leading the family readiness group, and helping the other family members anytime something would come up, etc. I had a lot going on.

When Mike got home from being gone for a year, I really had to remind myself that I was willingly handing him most of the load of the family. Anytime I would feel like I had to do everything, it was a good reminder that Mike was there and was happy to help. It was not because Mike was waiting on me to serve him. I had just gotten used to doing everything on my own. I didn't want to, but I was put in the situation where I had to.

Mike didn't deploy by choice or even volunteer. He went because he gave his word that he would if his unit was ever called up. He is a man of integrity.

If you are wondering if I have struggled with Mike being in charge, the answer is yes…however, that was due to insecurities on my part. I can honestly say it was not due to anything Mike had done.

Let me ask you this… did you get used to doing everything in your prior marriage?

Often women don't realize how they are part of the problem. To this, I would encourage you to keep track of how often you step in and find the solution to an issue without your husband. If it is more often than not, train yourself to talk through it with him. Asking for help is one of the healthiest things you can do. Let your husband help. That said, be willing to compromise if his solution is not the exact way you would handle it.

I have also noticed that some things women think about men are a result of what they have seen on TV or an assumption they have made due to what another woman has said. Did you know if you start with a false premise in science, you will come up with a false conclusion? Did you further know that the same is true when it comes to how women see men in our culture now?

Think about it, how often on a TV show or movie do you see the man depicted as lazy and stupid? How often does either the woman or the children have to swoop in and save the day? I am sorry to say more often than not...

This is done by design. The sooner you can make what has been viewed in the past as right and wrong now be viewed as anything goes, you can get people to do anything you want. Satan is no dummy. He is looking to destroy the family. Your family, my family, everyone's family. Because if he can, then there are no longer any absolutes.

Our culture and the mindset given to us by unqualified people are getting worse by the day. Speaking of unqualified people, I do want to mention that the people around you may have strong opinions about what does and doesn't work in a blended family, even if they don't live in one. Don't listen to them.

Also, be very cautious of professionals you listen to in the blended family counseling space too. If they are not personally in a blended family, I would be careful about taking advice from them.

It is kinda like someone who is not allowed to get married (priests) giving pre-marriage counseling to couples. What in the world do they know about marriage if they haven't been married? Basically, they have been told they know something...

It is time we all do what we can to stop taking part in the brainwashing. Start noticing inconsistencies and lies.

Stop allowing Hollywood to influence how you see things. Instead, allow God to show you how He set things up and why. Allow him to define the terms. Like myself, you will find peace and joy that you never knew before. You might still go through hardships, but you also will have a new way to communicate directly with Him.

Your family can only get to the level you are at. As harsh as that may sound, you have the ability to change directions. You and your spouse have the ability to make a beautiful love story still. All you have to do is make the decision and stick to it no matter what. You have the ability to do a better job than Mike & I have in some areas because we tell you exactly where we went wrong. We can tell you what will and won't work.

Without a doubt, I can tell you if you follow our suggestions… you too can make your remarriage your last marriage. The only question now is, will you?

Introduction

My name is Mike Baker.

I have been married almost 29 years, and we are a blended family.

I am a veteran, a plumber, a public speaker, an author, a podcaster, and an entrepreneur at heart.

Above all, I am a Christian.

I was raised by an alcoholic father. Dad reminded me every day that I was not smart, so when I left the house, I was convinced that I was the dumbest man to walk the earth.

My dad and I did not start to get along until roughly two years before he died.

You can't fix 20 years of trauma and abuse in two years.

I very much wanted to like or even love my dad, but it was hard. I could tell you that he made it hard, but once you become an adult that is on you. It was indeed my choice.

I married at 19 to a woman very much like my dad. Now to be fair you're only getting one side of the story. I made my share of mistakes, but I was always faithful.

That marriage ended miserably, and with two kids who were most definitely caught in the middle.

She would spend the remainder of her time convincing them how evil Brenda was and, at one point admitted that she let my sons do things I wouldn't so they would like her more.

I married a second time to a girl I truly loved, but apparently, couldn't really love me back.

We were married three months when she looked at me one day and told me I was a really great husband, but she didn't like being married.

She dragged me through two months of literal hell just after the wedding to tell me that.

She packed her stuff and went back to Cali to live with her mom and dad, and I tried to pick up the pieces.

One day at work as my second divorce was going through I was doing some work in a local rest home (I was the oxygen guy).

A young lady stopped me in the hallway to ask me if I would like to go to her company Christmas party, which was in January.

I asked if she knew my situation, and she did. I can't help but remember thinking, "Why would this girl want anything to do with me? I am obviously not worth it."

But I said I would, and off to the party we went.

Did I mention when I went to pick her up, I met her son?

The son she didn't tell me about.

I had no problem with this. I understood why she didn't say anything. She wanted to see if I was just there to get something from her like men before me, or if I was the real deal.

I have met so many men who put down single moms.

Shame on them. Don't claim Christ if you're going to have that type of attitude!

We were married 8 months later.

And here we are almost three decades later, still very much in love, and best friends.

Blended families are still families.

We have endured visits to Child Protective Services.

We were kept from my sons for over nine months due to false allegations by my ex.

We have been accused of things publicly via the newspaper by my wife's ex in-laws.

We have been in court with in-laws and both Ex's at the same time.

False allegation after false allegation, But we made it.

Where are we now?

Our two oldest sons are from my first marriage. They chose to believe my ex-wife's lies and have cut contact with my wife and me, even though it was primarily our house they grew up in.

This hurts my heart every day.

I adopted my wife's son, and we had two more.

We are very close with these three, their significant others, and their kids.

Since the kids moved out and on with their lives, my mom, who was also a piece of work, wrote us off when we told her that her behavior towards my wife was not acceptable.

That was a few years ago.

I always knew my dad had other kids, so I tracked them down.

Four sons and one daughter.

Two of my brothers died before I found them. The other two brothers and my sister want nothing to do with me because my dad left them -not because I did anything, but because my dad wronged them.

So I have been rejected by my mom, 2 of my sons, and my siblings.

Why do I tell you this?

Because you need to know family is messy, especially when you are trying to do the right thing.

I had a moment when I divorced my first wife when I was not a good dad. I didn't know what I was doing. I could barely take care of myself, but I learned.

The things I learned the most:

1. Be consistent

2. Know why you believe what you believe.

3. Be willing to take the arrows

This book is written to give you hope, as a man, in your relationship.

It is here to remind you that you won't win every battle, but you can win the war.

It will also help you to let go of those who would hinder that dream.

Blended families are still families. My goal is for your marriage to be your last marriage.

Today's world has so much noise. So many things that drown out the joy. Things that make it seem like the world may end tomorrow.

It used to be that religion and politics were just annoying topics that every family's "Uncle Phil" brought up at family functions and BBQ's, but it has turned into so much more.

Now families divide over it, to the point of no contact, essentially stealing the joy from the very fabric of the family.

Saying that the family is under attack would be an understatement, to say the least!

This is why my wife and I work in this space - the blended family space.

It's why we are passionate about saying the hard things and maybe hurting some feelings along the way.

But if we didn't care, we would just let your marriage implode.

God has given us a great gift in the institution of marriage, and there are currently major movements against it.

The world wants you to fail! It wants you to abandon God and follow your "heart" or my personal favorite "your truth".

We Christians (if you are a Christian) are the very last bastion of hope for the world. We hold answers in scripture, in our lives, in our families, and our very marriages that they desperately need. But they don't always realize they need it, do they?

My wife and I have been married almost 29 years at this point, and she is still my best friend. I don't mean like a roommate best friend, where we do everything together, and are never what married couples should be.

I mean we are everything a married couple should be.

Now this isn't to be arrogant.

This was the result of years of dedication to a singular cause: our marriage.

It meant hard choices and even harder decisions. It meant holding boundaries and apologizing when we crossed them.

It meant taking our vows of "for better or for worse" seriously, to the point of obsession.

Marriage is not temporary. Although life may be, we must treat marriage as though it's forever.

Marriage is the representation of Christ and his Bride.

Ephesians 5:25 "Husbands, love your wives, just as Christ also loved the church and gave Himself up for her."

Gave himself up for her. Like, gave His life. Now I know this may seem plain to you, but it is plain to others when they see you and your wife together. Do they see Christ in you to the point of death if necessary for this woman you have committed yourself to?

Or do they just hear your complaints?

"Happy wife, Happy life they say."

Run as far away from this statement as you can. It's not Godly, and it is not found in scripture, and it ruins marriages by the thousands every day.

But if you're like most men your attention is already starting to wane.

So, let's get to it, shall we?

There are three things men search for answers to on the internet when it comes to blended families.

1. Building Relationships with Stepchildren

2. Managing Parenting and Discipline

3. Navigating Co-parenting

I would submit to you a fourth that is not looked for but is the core fire of the problem.

4. Martial Relationship (this should be #1)

Number four is the key to the other three, but to be thorough, I am going to answer the other three first to set the stage for number four.

The first three are smaller fires. They are the distraction that comes with our intention to make this marriage work.

So why would we let distraction guide us?

1 Peter 5:8 "Be of sober spirit, be on the alert. Your adversary, the devil, prowls around like a roaring lion, seeking someone to devour."

Satan, that's why.

We have become wise in our own eyes, and we turn to the internet for solutions when the answer is in the bible that lays collecting dust on our shelves.

We claim God with our mouths, but not with our actions or even our lives.

Have you ever wondered why you have similar problems in a lot of your relationships? We tend to forget the most common denominator in that equation is us!

Oh, but that couldn't be a problem for us. It must be a common woman problem, right?

Passing the buck for an issue that is indeed our own will only push our problem further down the line and continue to keep us from the glory God desires us to have.

Remember Peter told us to "be on the alert". That means that we must watch out for issues within ourselves, as well as outside ourselves.

When I was 19 years old, I married my first wife.

A decision that would rock my world in the worst way for the rest of my life.

I remember thinking "I'm going to marry her" and at the time, I thought it was because I loved her. In truth, it was because I didn't love myself.

I had a terrible relationship with my Dad. He was mean, and an abusive alcoholic who belittled me my entire life. He literally told me I was dumb almost everyday till I moved out, and as a result I felt I was the lowest form of trash, with no future, to ever walk the earth. It took me years of my life to begin to see my worth.

My Dad and I didn't even remotely get along until the last couple of years before he died. A couple of years is not long enough for men over twenty broken.

Of course, I wish we had more time.

Point here is that my "wife-to-be" was just like him.

She was mean and caustic to most around her. She was a certified narcissist. Never wrong about anything. The blame for most things was placed, by her, squarely upon my shoulders.

After 2 kids and her cheating a couple of times, all in the span of two and half years, she left me for her last affair.

Let me be clear, you are truly only getting half of the story.

In all fairness I did not handle everything as well as I could have.

I had my share of the blame.

I struggled to provide for my family. I mean after all the only example I had to draw from was my Dad. Most people would avoid me growing up because of my Dad, so I had a pathetic foundation on what a husband and father looked like at best.

I was not my Dad. I am by nature, laid back. By character definition I would be considered an Omega male.

I didn't know how to stick up for myself, and why should I? I wasn't worth it, remember.

So back to when I wanted to marry her. I also remember thinking that I wanted at least one person to come to me and tell me that I shouldn't marry her.

You heard that right. I needed at least one person in my life to tell me "Don't do it!"

But none did. Not my mom and dad. Not my best friend at the time. Nobody spoke up.

Point is I knew it was a bad idea, but I also had the idea that this was all I was worth.

That choice haunted me more after the divorce than it did during the marriage.

I was not "alert" as I should have been, and I was not good about healthy boundaries in my life.

Life is 0% what happens to you, and 100% how you react. This is so true.

I am not the same man today.

1. **Building Relationships with Stepchildren**

   Let's be honest, this can be one of the most daunting tasks in the relationship. I once heard that it takes a kid half as much as they are old to accept a stepparent as a parental figure.

   Meaning that if a kid is 14 when the couple marries, then it will take roughly seven years for that kid to fully accept you in that role.

   Now, don't let those numbers discourage you. I have seen this in action, and I would agree with these numbers.

But here's the thing -you're in it for the long haul, right? You've got this!

Here's the problem I've seen with this scenario, and probably the biggest obstacle to building a solid relationship with your stepkids: **They're her kids.**

There I said it!

The idea of "yours and mine" is one of the single biggest killers of relationships in the blended family household. Too many couples enter the relationship treating the family unit like anything but a family.

Let me be clear: this is not a business merger; it's a blended family - **your family.**

Deuteronomy 6: 5-9

5 And you shall love the Lord your God with all your heart and with all your soul and with all your strength.

6 These words, which I am commanding you today, shall be on your heart.

7 And you shall repeat them diligently to your sons and speak of them when you sit in your house, when you walk on the road, when you lie down, and when you get up.

8 You shall also tie them as a sign to your hand, and they shall be as frontlets on your forehead.

9 You shall also write them on the doorposts of your house and on your gates.

This was advice given to the jews that absolutely still applies today.

Notice there is no differentiation between blended families and regular first-time marriages. **Family is family.**

What's the point? Quit treating these kids like they aren't yours.

It doesn't matter if they call you by your first name. In your house, you hold the office of husband and dad. You are the guy responsible for the family's direction and wellbeing. **Act like it!**

Nobody is going to die because you chose to treat those kids as if they were yours. Because they are!

Now here is where it gets spicy.

If you came into the relationship not willing to treat these kids with the same love and gratitude you would treat your own kids, you were wrong. **Own it!**

These kids may be fathered by someone else, but they are now lucky enough to be loved by you as well.

This does not fly in the face of the bio-parent. It helps them. More teamwork can be accomplished between the households in more amicable circumstances.

Yes, I understand that many circumstances are not amicable, but don't you think that kid deserves a place where the atmosphere is accepting and has healthy boundaries.

In the blended family area especially, these kids need to know you have their back.

Maybe your spouse gets in the way of the relationship by telling you it's not your kid, so it's not your worry.

That's not gonna work either.

I will repeat it again. You are still a family!

Maybe she refuses to let you discipline. We will get into that in later chapters.

Maybe you need some help with picking a spouse.

This is where things can break down.

Momma wants it done this way, and you want it done the other way.

Well, if you are claiming a Christian home then it's time to turn to God's word and come together in agreement of what that home will look according to scripture.

So, what's the key to building strong relationships with your stepkids?

Building a great relationship with your spouse.

Giving that kid an example to follow in what a relationship should look like and how a man treats the number one person in his life.

You caught that, right?

Your spouse must be the number one person in your life, or none of this will work.

We will get into that further in section four.

I feel it necessary at this point to say **you are the lynchpin** in this.

Are you spending quality time with the stepkids A.K.A your kids now too?

Are you listening to what their needs could be? Do you hear them, or do they just annoy you?

If you listen closely, the answers are there.

Deuteronomy 6 is plain: the teaching and caring never stop.

Side note:

After almost 29 years, I can confidently say my marriage is flourishing.

I always put my family first. Always put their needs before my own.

Both my bio-kids and my step kid got equal "Dad" time, to the best of my ability.

I worked a lot but made family my priority.

With that said,

You're not always going to win.

Yesterday, I met an 80-year-old man yesterday who told me through tear-filled eyes, about his divorce many years before, and how his ex-spouse had actively poisoned his kids against him.

His kids went no-contact.

It's been over thirty years since he has seen or talked to them, and it breaks his heart.

Sometimes you put in the reps and lose.

Why am I telling you this?

James 4:17

"So, for one who knows the right thing to do and does not do it, for him it is sin."

This is a powerful statement, so let it settle in.

Sometimes there is an ROI (or in this case ROE- Return On Experience), but not always.

1 Corinthians 13: 4-8

4 Love is patient, love is kind, it is not jealous; love does not brag, it is not arrogant.

5 It does not act disgracefully, it does not seek its own benefit; it is not provoked,

does not keep an account of a wrong suffered,

6 it does not rejoice in unrighteousness but rejoices with the truth.

7 it keeps every confidence, it believes all things, hopes all things, endures all things.

8 Love never fails

Here's the point.

When building relationships with your stepkids, you must always do three things.

1. Love their mom with all your being (Section 4)

2. Love them like your own, because love never fails

3. Do the right thing, because it's the right thing

You won't always win, and sometimes those losses will make you question everything you've done and everything you have invested into the relationship.

But can you look back and say, **"I did everything I could"?**

I would submit to you that success is possible in these relationships even when there is failure.

2.   Managing Parenting and Discipline

Now we are into a subject that raises ire and defensiveness.

You can tell people how they should and shouldn't spend their money. You can tell them they look fat in those pants.

But tell them how to discipline their kids…Watch out! The fight is coming.

Truth is, we all make mistakes.

I made huge mistakes in parenting and discipline when my kids were younger. But I also made some great decisions and got some things very right.

Trial and error are part of the game.

I always felt bad for the oldest child. That poor kid was the crash test dummy for parenting ideas. LOL

I myself don't have a problem with spanking, but I also think there is a tremendous difference between spanking and abuse.

So, in this book, I may endorse spanking, but I am never referring to abuse when I say that.

With that, there are many couples within the church that have moved toward "natural parenting."

"Natural parenting, also known as attachment parenting, is a philosophy and approach to child-rearing that emphasizes nurturing, bonding, and responding to a child's needs in a natural and intuitive way. This method often incorporates elements from traditional and instinctive practices that have been used for centuries.

Engaging with children in a respectful and empathetic manner, listening to their feelings and needs, and guiding them with understanding rather than authoritarian methods."

This is a "child-first" idea, or more specifically a "child-centered" idea.

This is not scripture.

This is man's answer to your parenting dilemma.

And so called "Christians" are following it.

I can assure you that if you are using this method, it will backfire and blow up in your face.

Natural parenting does not teach them to fear God or think of others (due to its child-centered nature).

Scripture says In Proverbs 22:6

"Train up a child in the way he should go,

Even when he grows older, he will not abandon it."

There's a tremendous difference between training and guiding.

They are not the same.

"Training" involves a certain level of pain in the learning, where the continued effort eventually leads to the right outcome, but only through a series of frustrated attempts to get there.

"Guiding", in the respect used under natural parenting, means you take away the pain of learning, and do the hard parts for them. This only teaches them that you are going to pick up the slack.

This leads to entitlement.

Why should they do it, if you're just going to come behind and do it for them anyway?

Look, God said you are a family.

It's time for you to create an atmosphere in which, when the kids are there, they are active participants in the family unit.

So, let's talk about something that no counselor will bring up. **Family Identity.**

This could be one of the single biggest tools available to you as a father.

We set the tone for the family. We are the timekeepers.

Once again, I want you to toss out the "Happy wife, happy life" nonsense. It's not in scripture. You know what is in scripture?

Proverbs 21:9

"It is better to live on a corner of a roof Than in a house shared with a contentious woman"

Proverbs 21:19

"It is better to live in a desert land Than with a contentious and irritating woman"

Proverbs 25:24

"It is better to live on a corner of the roof, than in a house shared with a contentious woman."

Proverbs 27:15

"A constant dripping on a day of steady rain and a contentious woman are alike"

I think you get the point.

The "happy wife, happy life" mantra leads to a relationship that you survive in, not thrive in.

It's ok for you to take up the mantle of being in charge, but not being a dictator.

Family identity is the tool for that process.

It's also a great tool to get you and your spouse on the same page, moving in the same direction.

So what is Family identity?

"Family identity is the environment parents create and maintain within their family that reflect their family goals and values."

Family identity is a powerful tool for creating.

When God created the earth, He put man in charge of all things and told us to subdue it. He gave us a creative spirit in which to do that. This is the same creative spirit we bring to family identity in its goals and values.

As a kid, it didn't take me long to figure out that people either loved or hated my alcoholic father.

Dad was the life of the party or ready to go to fists in a heartbeat. He was angry and negative.

I mentioned this earlier. Why do I bring it up again?

My dad set a family identity that the "Baker Family' was to be avoided. That we were less than desirable, and you need not give us your time.

Mom was the beatdown wife, and I was the scraggly kid who was handful because I was scared of everything.

I was scared to fail.

I was scared to do anything that would rock the boat.

I was terrified of my dad, convinced that the wrong word would send me to the hospital.

Let me be clear though. Dad wasn't the type of violent you see in the movies.

There were instances of violence, but not necessarily constant violence.

What there was, was the constant threat of violence.

My dad kept me under his thumb enough to keep me scared. This was my family Identity: Be anything, but don't be a Baker.

We changed that in our blended family.

I told my wife that being a Baker, from the day of our marriage forward, would be a great and glorious thing.

To this day, that is the identity my kids carry on in their families.

If done right, it will set a tone for discipline that is expected and a level of parenting that is consistent between both mom and dad.

So how do you create Family identity?

It's simple.

Sit down as a couple - no kids - and mind map all the things you would like for your family.

Don't know what mind mapping is?

It's simple. All your ideas, no matter how far-fetched, or ridiculous, or outlandish, big, or small, go on a piece of paper. Not enough? Use as many as you need.

Then you begin to sort. Have fun with the process.

Maybe what you want is to travel more as a family. That could be anything from a trip to Europe to a few camping trips in the summer.

This would go down in your family identity as a family that travels together, enjoys each other on the open road, and laughs at each other during silly car or plane rides.

The possibilities for family identity are endless.

What was ours?

Nothing beats being a Baker!

We are the helpers. We care and we work together.

We are family, and when others abandon us, we never abandon each other.

We hug, no matter the age, and we cry only when it's appropriate.

We are strong, entrepreneurial, hardworking, and above all, children of God!

My Dad instilled unhealthy fear and loathing into me.

My wife and I countered our upbringings by instilling a kind heart, a loving home, and telling those boys they could be or do anything.

Don't get me wrong.

I believe it's scriptural for kids to have a healthy fear of their parents. It's the same fear we have of the Father.

This is the way we instill discipline.

Time-outs are nothing but a rest between boxing rounds.

Reasoning with a two-year-old is like speaking Greek to a Russian. In your head it's reasonable.

In reality, it's a complete waste of time.

The very nature of punishment is to correct poor or inappropriate behavior. In many instances it is for safety reasons.

This is why we create an environment within the home in which a child can fail under supervision.

In the home, he can pick up the pieces with love and correction from you and your wife.

2 Timothy 3:16

"All Scripture is inspired by God and beneficial for teaching, for rebuke, for correction, for training in righteousness."

What does this mean?

It means the home is also a place for us to make mistakes in an environment that is safe for us. An environment that allows us to humble ourselves and keep ourselves in check as well.

The key to discipline is to not be afraid of it.

Here is the formula my wife and I have used for years when it came to discipline of kids or grandkids:

Punishment > ETDIRTFT

This should thoroughly confuse you.

Here it is. Punishment must be greater than the **E**ffort **T**o **D**o **I**t **R**ight **T**he **F**irst **T**ime.

You are hindering your kid's growth by going easy.

For the most part, remember I told you that you are still a family, blended family or not, and all the rules we just talked about apply.

There really aren't that many extra rules with new kids, but they carry some weight.

1. Never expect your step kid to just accept you. That takes time and effort with no guaranteed results. You must do the right thing because it's the right thing. God is watching. Give him a reason to bless the relationship.

2. Never introduce the step kid as "the step kid". Simply introduce them by their name, as you would any of your kids. The term by itself can be demeaning to a kid who isn't even sure they want anything to do with you.

3. Never, and I mean never, show preference between bio-kids and step-kids. You chose this relationship. Put your big boy pants on and own the family - it's your after all.

4. Never belittle either ex-spouse to the kids -any of the kids - no matter how much you want to. To be honest, I did this in the beginning, and it never ended well. I always apologized.

5. This is far from last, but you establish that if you are king in this household then mom is queen, and treat her as such. Your kids need to know you mean business in

this area, and her kids need to see a man actually love their mom.

We will touch more on number 5 in section 4-The Marital relationship.

3. **Navigating Co-parenting**

This section may be hard for you to swallow.

Most exes never fully come to a great and understanding relationship in the area of co-parenting.

Sure, you see the ones on TikTok and Facebook that some make their parenting plans work.

And then you hear a podcast or maybe read a book by two women -an ex and a stepmom- that are best friends, and life is rosy for them.

These scenarios happen. It is possible, and I pray that it's yours.

However, after helping and counseling blended families for 20+ years, I can tell you that two types of parenting exist.

The smaller of the two you are already familiar with.

Co-parenting - a relationship in which all spouses and/or significant others conduct themselves appropriately with the kids in mind and do indeed discuss most everything.

Then there's the other where most people, both believers and unbelievers, live.

Parental Management- the situation in which you pick your battles wisely because there will always be one, and you spend the bulk of your time managing all the missiles fired from your ex.

This Is not ideal, but here are some suggestions that should help.

1. **Your house is your house!** Outside of neglect and abuse, you can't do anything about what your ex or your wife's ex is doing within the four walls of his or her home, so don't try.

2. **Your rules are your rules!** If you're supposed to keep your nose out of your ex's house, then also keep her out of yours. What happens within your four walls has nothing to do with her. Keep her out of it. This goes for your wife's ex as well.

3. **Matthew 5:44** "But I say to you, love your enemies and pray for those who persecute you". Does this one really need explaining?

4. **Don't be petty!** Take a step back and remember the tantrums and the drama brought on by exes say more

about them then you (unless you're that person). Let it roll off. Take a deep breath and move on with your day.

5. **Don't drag the kids into the fight.** Use yourself as a shield for those kids, both bio and step. You're an adult. You can take it.

6. **Never allow disrespect to your spouse.** This can be tricky but must be done. I'm not suggesting fights in the alley, but you do need to be firm. Protect that woman you chose, and let the kids see you do it!

Parental management doesn't have to be life-ending or life-altering. It needs to be smart and efficient.

Don't hang out during kid drops.

Don't get sucked into meaningless arguments.

Don't allow yourself to get suckered by insults. Nod and move on.

Self-control is more valuable than you know.

And never compromise your convictions as a Christian!

A bitter ex will always go for the throat, but you know that, so don't expose it.

Both step kids and bio kids will many times, at the manipulation of the angry ex, engage in this behavior as well.

Please note to yourself that this is not personal. They can say some awful things, but they are lashing out for reasons you may be involved in but are not your fault.

Let's talk now about the dark side of co-parenting.

Deuteronomy 6 talks about teaching your kids. It never gives you a guarantee that they want to learn at the time, but it does tell you what's necessary to get the message through.

Proverbs 22:6

"Train up a child in the way he should go, even when he grows older he will not abandon it."

This was my mantra with the boys when they were growing up, but two things occurred to me when the boys moved out.

1. Older is not necessarily 18. We tell ourselves that this "older" reference is when they move out, but really, it's

pretty nondescript. This could be anytime after they are out. 18-80. We just don't know.

2. As much as we want to see a guarantee here, there isn't one. We cannot see what God sees. We teach, train, and test so that when that kid leaves the house, they have a toolbox for life. We cannot guarantee that they will ever use it (especially if we are not). We can only make sure they have it.

This is where the no-contact conversation happens.

Colossians 3:21

"Fathers, do not exasperate your children, so that they will not lose heart."

This is where we will feel utter failure. Is it our fault that the kid quit the family?

Were we too hard or too soft? Did we not offer enough compassion and flexibility?

What did we do? How is this our fault?

Let me be very transparent about my experience.

We have five boys- two from my first marriage, one from my wife's first marriage, and two that are ours.

I received a phone call one day from my wife's ex.

He was thousands of dollars behind in child support, and to be honest I was waiting for this call. This guy and his parents had taken us to court in different cases, at the same time, accusing my wife and I of all kinds of abuse and neglect.

Anything to cause a problem, both financially and in my wife's and my relationship.

He wanted to know if he signed away his parental rights and signed off on my adoption of my stepson, would we forgive the back child support?

I didn't hesitate to accept

On the other side, I had my very caustic ex taking us to court for the same types of things.

Where we lived at the time, the burden of proof lay upon the accused, not the accuser. Meaning all they had to do was file a piece of paper with accusations to the court and we had to prove it wasn't true.

All the while, my wife and I are trying to create this family identity and unit within our home.

We doubled down on our relationship and took the arrows best we could.

Amidst the thousands of dollars in court and lawyer fees, we stood strong together, but not without its cost.

During my first deployment to Iraq, my wife informed me that my second oldest was having issues.

When I came home on leave, he informed me that he wanted to move in with his mom.

This was devastating to me. My wife, who was a stay-at-home mom, had put thousands of hours of love and attention into this kid. Treated him like he was her own, tried to teach him work ethic.

He turned his back on all of it, because he believed that grass was greener at moms.

My ex, at one point, legitimately told me that she would purposefully let the boys do things at her house they were not allowed to do at mine so they would like her more, and she was proud of it.

That son hasn't talked to us in over 15 years now.

What's my point here?

There are no guarantees for a positive outcome.

No guarantees that someone who is bitter and angry won't dedicate themselves to the destruction of your home and the relationships therein.

No guarantee that all of your hard work, and sweat, compromise, and prayer will feel like it all came to nothing.

No guarantee that you don't question yourself everyday for the decisions you have made in the past and how those will affect your future.

No guarantees, except one.

James 4:17

"So, for one who knows the right thing to do and does not do it, for him it is sin."

The right thing to do is always the right thing to do.

James 1: 2-4

"2 Consider it all joy, my brothers and sisters, when you encounter various trials,

3 knowing that the testing of your faith produces endurance.

4 And let endurance have its perfect result, so that you may be perfect and complete, lacking in nothing."

How do we consider it all joy?

Keep it in perspective and keep it in prayer!

Since that day with my second oldest, my oldest has also gone no contact with me.

These things hurt my heart every day. Every day I think about my sons who have frivolously given up what could have been some of the most important relationships of their lives.

My other three sons and my wife and I have a great relationship.

Did I mention that my oldest two sons essentially went no-contact with not just me and my wife but their brothers and our whole side of the family?

Like I said no guarantees except in Christ.

Obviously, ours was considerably more of a "parental management" scenario than not. So how did my wife and I manage to survive the missiles, and the siege brought against our new family from all sides?

1. First, we leaned toward God

2. We leaned into our relationship, not away from it

And this is where we get into what is the most important part of this small book.

Your marriage!

4. The Maritial relationship

When we stand at the marriage altar as men, we feel a great relief and a great nervousness.

We anticipate the night to come, and we feel the happiness in the moment.

Of course, everything is great then- it's a wedding!

Everyone smiles, everyone is mostly in a good mood, and most importantly, everything is possible.

Fast forward a few years.

You're now at each other's throats. You are unsure who this person is because she no longer looks like the woman you married, and through a chain of unfortunate events, you end up in a bitter divorce.

Sometimes very bitter.

God created marriage to be a blessing to us, ultimately to be a representation of Christ and His Bride, the Church.

Ephesians 5:25

"Husbands, love your wives, just as Christ also loved the church and gave Himself up for her"

The man was meant to be the head from the very beginning, and scripture is very clear on this- but not the dictatorial kind.

The world today has most definitely skewed that image.

1 Corinthians 11:3

"But I want you to understand that Christ is the head of every man, and the man is the head of a woman, and God is the head of Christ"

We as men have three core things that we need to do in the marriage- three core responsibilities:

1. Serve

2. Provide

3. Lead

Yes, that is the right order.

We take the last of what's available. We give until it hurts, and we guide our families to success.

Whether through work, relationships or play, they come first.

Now you have come to the altar again.

This is it! She is the one.

You didn't really picture yourself here again, but here you are. Same joy. Same smiles.

Fast forward a bit and now there are problems brewing again.

Problems very similar to the last marriage.

"What is going on!?", you ask yourself.

Let me tell you- you are going on.

The only consistent thing in this scenario is you.

It's not that all women are the same, it's that you haven't changed. Maybe you haven't accepted your part of what happened in the last failed marriage.

Maybe it's the fact that when you're standing amongst friends and family, totally enthralled in the joy of the moment, and you state those eternal words "for better or for worse", it doesn't occur to you what worse looks like.

And there it is. "Worse" has no defined depth anymore than joy does.

Yet we think that every day should be moonlight and roses, and we buy the lie that if this were really love, it should be easy.

I mean, after all, Joe up the street seems to have a great marriage, until he doesn't.

That guy at work is always talking about how great things are at home, until he isn't.

What do I mean?

We have become a society that shames others and ourselves when our relationships begin to get hard.

This is the age of no-contact.

Never have we been so connected to people around the world, and yet so disconnected in our relationships. We smugly write off family members because we no longer agree biblically or politically.

The truth is, relationships are messier now then they have been in a long, long time.

One of the first keys to a successful re-marriage is ownership.

Ownership of our faults. Ownership of our roles as husbands. Ownership of our roles as fathers. And especially ownership of our faith.

So, let's dive into the first of our three core responsibilities- **Serve.**

To Serve is to be transparent. It's to be always available, both mentally and physically.

To Serve is the true heart of a King that desires success for his kingdom and his subjects.

So, let's talk about numbers.

Currently according to CDC data, 42% of all marriages are likely to end in divorce.

But let's break that down.

- 41% of first marriages fail.
- 60% of second marriages fail (a lot in part due to the extra baggage).

- 73% of 3+ marriages end in divorce.

How about we break it down just a bit more?...

- Couples who cohabitate (live together) are 1.31 times more likely to divorce.
- Couples who attend church regularly have a divorce rate 25-50% lower than non-churchgoers.
- Divorce for virgins is about 50% lower than those who had premarital sex.
- Lastly, the divorce rate increases substantially for those who have had

multiple sexual partners (apparently, body count does matter).

What does this have to do with serving?

Everything!

You can't run a business or a marriage without knowing what you're up against.

The odds say you are more likely to fail than to succeed, and many times we fall into the "maybe it's just not meant to be" trap.

We fool ourselves into thinking that maybe this isn't God's will for me.

That's just straight up cowardice and selfishness talking.

Ephesians 5:28

"So husbands also ought to love their own wives as their own bodies. He who loves his own wife loves himself"

Of course, this makes sense when held to

Genesis 2:24:

"For this reason, a man shall leave his father and his mother, and be joined to his wife; and they shall become one flesh"

These become tied together even more via

Ephesians 5:25:

"Husbands, love your wives, just as Christ also loved the church and gave Himself up for her"

The Problem with blended families and re-marriage overall is that we have a skewed picture.

I once heard it said that the funny thing about the white speck on top of chicken poop, is that it's chicken poop too.

What does that mean? Just because it looks different, or we choose to perceive it as different, doesn't mean it is.

Blended families are still families, and the same rules for all families apply!

Same with marriage. Remarriage is still marriage, and the same rules apply.

Just because it may "feel" different, or because there's more baggage involved, doesn't mean the rules shift for you.

The great thing is that the answer you seek is still there, and that's encouraging!

1 Timothy 5:8

"But if anyone does not provide for his own, and especially for those of his household, he has denied the faith and is worse than an unbeliever."

This is where the rubber meets the road! This is non-negotiable according to scripture.

This is serving.

"But Mike I do this already", I can hear the men in the front say.

Do you? Do you really serve your wife and your family in such a way that you are honoring the "one flesh" rule of marriage, and you are serving at the highest level, making sure that you show Christ in all things?

If you were, we wouldn't be having this conversation.

So, what tools do I have for you?

Proverbs 23:7

"For as he thinks within himself, so he is"

This is one of the most powerful statements in scripture!

If you feel like a failure, you are.

If you feel like a winner, you are.

If you feel _____, you are (fill in the blank).

What are you doing about your mindset every day?

Prayer is the first tool. It's what makes you or breaks you. The further from prayer we get, the more we rely on ourselves, and we have already seen that we cannot manage ourselves very well. We need the Father.

Prayer time is not a hard, fast time-and-place rule or type of activity.

We see prayer happening all over scripture at all times of the day and night.

Same goes for us. Anytime is truly a good time, but we need the habit.

So right now, put this book down, go to your phone and set an alarm for whatever time of day you think you have available for prayer. It's that simple.

Go to your Father and ask for the help in your marriage and family that you need.

If you are truly in Christ, He WILL answer the call. This isn't a long-distance relationship. If you are truly a Christian, God is always with you.

See, this seems like basic stuff, but most of you have wandered, or you have decided that because prayer is such a simple and easy activity, that it just doesn't have any power.

That is nothing but arrogance talking, and you need to expel it as quickly as possible.

A note on **time:** I get that everyone has a busy schedule, but the important things must always be handled.

As we speak, I am writing this book at 3a.m. Why? Because it's that important. It's vital that you and I have a conversation. Sleep has become an excuse and a crutch to many. "Well, Mike, I need my 8 hrs". Nope, what you need to do is grow a set and be a man.

Men need to get things done. We don't get things done in slumber.

Proverbs 6: 9-11

"How long will you lie down, O sluggard? When will you arise from your sleep? 'A little sleep, a little slumber, A little folding of the hands to rest' Your poverty will come in like a vagabond and your need like an armed man."

All scripture is powerful, but this one should especially hit home for men.

Sleep is for people who can afford it.

That used to be a joke I would tell people, but as I get older, I find it to be more true than I originally thought.

And this brings us back to prayer.

Deuteronomy 6:7

"You shall teach them diligently to your sons and shall talk of them when you sit in your house and when you walk by the way and when you lie down and when you rise up."

Anytime! You can do it in the car before you come home during the day, or before you drive off. You can do it before bed or when you're going to bed.

A solid ten-minute talk with God multiple times during the day is just as good as sitting down to prayer for an hour. It's about creating the habit. This, in turn, will begin to shift the mindset.

Second tool is **Mindset.**

I'm going to give you a very personal example of how I overcame lustful thoughts in the beginning of my marriage. I embraced them.

Matthew 12: 43-45

"Now when the unclean spirit goes out of a man, it passes through waterless places seeking rest, and does not find it. Then it says, 'I will return to my house from which I came'; and when it comes, it finds it unoccupied, swept, and put in order. Then it goes and takes along with it seven other spirits more wicked than itself, and they go in and live there; and the last state of that man becomes worse than the first. That is the way it will also be with this evil generation."

There is a huge key here. If you wish to drop a sinful behavior, you must replace it with another behavior.

Same with mindset. If you wish to think something more positive you must replace the existing thought, not simply reject the negative thought. That is twice the work. Let the new thought do the work for you.

So how did I embrace lustful thoughts? (thought I was going to leave you hanging, didn't you?)

I made a shift. The problem wasn't the lustful thoughts. The problem was having those thoughts about other women.

Whether those women were walking down the street, in a magazine, or in a movie, it was scripturally sin for me to entertain those thoughts.

But not if they were about my wife.

I simply shifted those lustful thoughts to always be about my wife, and after a few months, I found that without effort I was fantasizing about her, and as an added result I became more infatuated with my wife and more focused on my bride.

Don't let your church convince you that this is bad practice. It's a powerful tool in keeping the important things important and helping keep your mindset on task.

Now this is just an example, and I will drive into the intimacy subject later. But this is a powerful tool.

Boundaries is another tool IN your toolbox-

To have a unified front with your spouse, you must have established the rules of "same page thinking".

As per Scripture, the buck stops with you, and you could use that to your advantage, but that doesn't mean it's to the family's advantage.

What do I mean?

I mean that you serve your wife and family to the point of death, if need be, but you also set the rules.

This means you must have boundaries in place.

Yes, I will fix the deck, but that's not the only project I need to work on this weekend.

Yes, I will take out the garbage, but I need to finish what I'm doing first. Yes, I will drop what I'm doing to help you, but that needs to be a theme for our whole family.

You are a **Servant King**, not a slave.

I'm not talking about being Hitler in the house about your time. I'm talking about training your wife, to a degree, about how you prefer your workflow so that you can maximize your ability to help her.

In turn, your wife really should be doing the same with you so that you can both work toward the same goals.

Hopefully, you understand the importance of what we have discussed so far in this section.

These are the things that begin to define who we are as husbands and leaders in the house, as well as in the church.

You don't think people notice in church, you say?

Think again!

Throughout my marriage, I have actively looked for men older than me who were qualified in their marriage to give me advice.

That is a tall order to fill a lot of times.

Many times, I have felt as though I am the only one pushing in a scriptural direction with my marriage.

That's not arrogance.

That's a results-based decision. Many may think it's judgmental to say such a thing, but when looking to another older Christian male for advice in my own marriage, I have to judge. Judgment is a tool that helps me find my level within my own marital relationship.

There are straight up, too many soft men within the church.

Many churches have left the door open to a soft version of feminism, and their marriages are suffering for it.

Never be afraid to look at another man's fruit within his marriage before asking for advice.

This is where yet another tool exists for you.

Find a **mentor** for your marriage.

We find mentors in business- why not our marriage as well?

The right mentor can add tremendous progress within your marriage, and be picky about who you ask.

What are their kids like?

How does their spouse interact with them?

How do they interact within the body of Christ?

Do he and his wife touch each other regularly?

Maybe you haven't noticed before, but watch couples in your church next time you're there. Do they ever touch?

Do they hold hands? Do they casually touch each other during conversations?

Do they sit together during church, or do they allow their kids to separate them on the row, for "management" reasons?

Do they even talk outside of simple requests?

There are so many tells in a relationship. You need only watch.

Be picky when it comes to finding a mentor.

Now we come to one of the most valuable pieces of advice I could possibly give you.

This may be the single most important piece of advice I give you in this book.

First, what have we covered?

1. Prayer as a tool

2. Mindset as a tool

3. Boundaries as a tool

4. Finding a mentor

5. ????

So, what is #5.

Choose your wife first!

Christ died for his bride. She was first and foremost on his mind, and we are all part of that bride, if indeed you are in Christ.

We have all heard the scenario: You, your wife and your child are on a boat.

Boat goes down.

You find yourself in a spot where you can see both your child and your spouse.

You can't get to both.

Who do you save?

You save the wife. Your wife is the right answer.

"To have and to hold, in sickness and in health, for richer or for poorer, from this day forward, till death do you part"

Sound familiar?

You pledged your life to this woman.

Now many of you have already rolled your eyes and come up with many excuses.

"My wife would want me to save our child!"

"I couldn't condemn a child like that Mike!"

"I would always pick the child!"

"But children are innocent, Mike!"

I have heard every reason under the sun for why husbands would abandon their wives for their kids.

Rarely Have I had a husband say to the wife.

The answer to save the child says so much more about your marriage than you might realize. For one, it says you're more than likely child centered.

What does that mean?

It means the kids are the center of the relationship.

How many parent will justify this with:

- "But their innocent"
- "But they need me"
- "But I want better for them"

These things may be true, but they do not trump marriage.

The greatest gift you can give your kids is a great marriage!

Teaching them what love between a man and woman should look like. So, when they seek spouses, they know what to look for because they first saw it at home within their own four walls.

Now I know you're still shaking your head thinking I'm wrong about this, but remember you're here looking for answers because your way may not be working so well.

Let me clarify.

I'm not talking about neglecting your kids. I'm talking about keeping the primary relationship the primary relationship.

You were husband and wife long before you were parents, and you will be long after the kids move out. If you think that you can give your marriage the time it needs when the kids are gone, I can tell you firsthand that rarely, if ever, happens.

When you sit in a restaurant and watch the old people eat, there are typically two types.

One couple sits in absolute silence without so much as a phone in their hand to occupy them. They just don't talk.

Of course there's the other kind- smiling, sitting in the same side of the booth, and continuously talking, and holding hands the whole while.

We all have the same thought when we see the second couple: "I hope my wife and I are like that when we get old." You should think that.

Here's a newsflash for you. The second couple spent their entire marriage working on the marriage.

The first couple spent their marriage managing kids, and now they just don't know each other.

They are two strangers sitting at the table.

Kids come second.

God, wife, kids

The relationship with your kids is subject to the primary relationship with your wife. If the primary is broken, the others are considerably more likely to be as well.

My wife and I have been married almost 29 years. She is still my best friend.

Still the only person I want to see at the beginning of my day and at its end.

I cannot imagine a world without her, and my sons know it.

We endured back-to-back-to-back-to-back court cases, visits from the police, endless talks with Child Protective Services, and divisive behavior from old friends at the congregation I had attended since I was 14.

All while I was working three jobs trying to make sure my wife could stay home to give our sons stability.

We still had a weekly date night. Even if all we could do was window-shop the mall or split a desert- we did it!

We still had couch time, where she and I would catch up on our day when I got home, and the boys were not allowed to interrupt. That was a half-hour each day.

We eventually took a vacation every year.

One year with the boys, and the next, just the two of us.

We worked on our marriage. Through blood, sweat, and tears, we forged a bond that no man can shake.

It was hard- very hard- but it was and still is my single greatest accomplishment.

Don't tell me you have no time.

Let's now talk about the most delicate of subjects- **Intimacy.**

So, a quick internet search rendered this:

"In studies on sexless marriages, it was found that the participants were about evenly divided between men and women. This indicates that both genders experience sexless marriages at similar rates. Participants in these studies ranged in age from 18 to 65, with the majority being in their late 30s to early 40s."

Participants were about evenly divided.

That doesn't line up with what men have been saying on the internet for a while.

Men have claimed to be the primary victims in this area.

What does it mean that they were evenly divided?

It means both sides are having a sex problem within the marriage.

It means we have forgotten how to serve and talk to each other. There is a thought out there (I don't know where it came from) that would suggest that if love is meant to be, it should be smooth and easy, even in the face of adversity.

What a bunch of crap!

Overall, here are the numbers for the lack of the act itself.

"Estimates suggest that between 15% to 20% of marriages are sexless, meaning couples engage in sexual activity fewer than ten times a year."

1 Corinthians 7: 3-5

"3 The husband must fulfill his duty to his wife, and likewise the wife also to her husband.

4 The wife does not have authority over her own body, but the husband does; and likewise, the husband also does not have authority over his own body, but the wife does.

5 Stop depriving one another, except by agreement for a time so that you may devote yourselves to prayer and come together again so that Satan will not tempt you because of your lack of self-control."

These scriptures seem straight forward. That act of intimacy, in as much as scripture covers it is expected.

So why am I telling you what you already know?

There's a good chance that if you're reading this you fall into that 15-20%

Heck, those numbers may be higher as most couples will not divulge that this is a problem in their marriage.

Blended family life is beyond stressful at times, but we don't have a corner in that market.

Regular first time marriages can have many of the same problems.

Remember what I said in the beginning?

Blended families are still families. We just have more luggage. So, let's get into the logistics of the issue.

Men are clueless in many respects, and women think saying something once is enough.

So many of these issues start as small, miniscule problems and blossom into major issues overnight.

What do men do?

We expect.

We think that by marriage rights alone, we are due sex.

That's not sex- that's just an orgasm.

If a woman does not feel needed and desired, she won't respond. If she thinks she's just another 'check off the box' part of your day, she won't respond.

If she sees you checking out other women, she won't respond.

If the only time you touch her is for sexy time, she won't respond.

If she feels like a burden or something you're trying to fit into your day, she won't respond.

If she doesn't feel listened to, she won't respond

I think you get the point.

A woman wants a man who will lead. This is true across the board.

I have talked with hundreds of women over the years about this very subject, and they all say the same thing. "If I could find a man worth following, I would follow him"

From the most feminist women I have met to the meekest. The same answer.

Problem is they don't think that man exists.

This is our fault as men.

We have decided that being sensitive to our wives' needs is somehow not masculine.

1 Peter 3:7

"You husbands in the same way, live with your wives in an understanding way, as with someone weaker, since she is a woman; and show her honor as a fellow heir of the grace of life, so that your prayers will not be hindered."

The Greek word for weaker is "asthenes (ἀσθενής, ές)" meaning: Not strong, physically or morally.

Now, God said this for a reason.

The point here is not that women are weak or inadequate. The point here is that in your vows, you pledged to take care of her at a level that might include giving your very life.

They were created weaker, but not without purpose.

They are the heart of the home, and we are the protectors. The heart by itself, exposed, is weak and open to harm, unless the muscle, sinew, and bone protect it.

Yet we treat women like they are us.

They are Not! Pull your head out and realize that what you have in your wife, frail as she may be, pumps the blood throughout your relationship that you need to survive and thrive.

A woman who feels supported and protected will do anything for you or with you, but not before you have proven your grit.

God is an excellent strategist.

He designed it this way to motivate men. Let's be honest, we are typically lazy by nature and would probably let our wives do everything if they let us.

God set this deal up to motivate us at our very core for the love of a woman.

This is why the marriage is representative of Christ and His Bride, the Church.

We have so much to gain by pouring ourselves into our marriage and, ultimately, our God.

Fix this, and you will fix your sex life, and it will take on a life of its own.

Some of you may feel it's too far gone to fix.

Maybe it is.

But it is never too far gone to try to fix.

When you stand before God on Judgement Day, do you really want to have to explain why you gave up?

Look, the answers are here if you really read what I am saying.

I have almost three decades of work on my marriage, and my marital sex life is still very much intact.

It's all about the simple things.

Like taking a bath- I still can't believe how many men want to engage their wives when they are filthy from the day.

Don't be a pig-clean up!

In Conclusion

We have talked about…

1. Building Relationships with Stepchildren
2. Managing Parenting and Discipline
3. Navigating Co-parenting
4. Marital Relationship

I have tried to keep this as simple as possible.

I have tried to put this in a manner that you can apply to your own life.

I want you to succeed. I want this marriage to be your last marriage, the one that carries you through to the end as one of the greatest joys in your life.

Don't buy the bull that it only happens to some men. That is simply not true.

It is available to all men who seek it, and make the necessary sacrifices expected of them according to God's word.

Don't be prideful, boastful, or arrogant.

Your job as a husband and father, according to the Word of God, will be the greatest training in leadership you ever receive.

And you will be accompanied by a mate that has your back every step of the way. Be a man worth following.

Next Steps:

1. Get yourself right with God according to the Bible as seen at the end of Chapter 1 in Brenda's section
2. Address the issues in your remarriage & work with your spouse
3. Join our Blended Family Momentum Group
4. Visit our site blendedfamilymomentum.com to purchase our video series
5. Subscribe to our YouTube Channel

   youtube.com/@momsmixedfamilyblender726

Milton Keynes UK
Ingram Content Group UK Ltd.
UKHW021452011224
451693UK00013B/1211

9 798992 024609